FIGURES OF A VOYAGE

Collected Poems
(1984–2000)

Cecilia Margaret Harding

ATHENA PRESS
MIAMI   LONDON

FIGURES OF A VOYAGE: *Collected Poems (1984–2000)*
Copyright © Cecilia Margaret Harding 2002

ISBN 1 930493 78 9

First Published 2002 by
ATHENA PRESS PUBLISHING CO.
1001 Brickell Bay Drive, Suite 2202
Miami, Florida 33131

Printed for Athena Press

FIGURES OF A VOYAGE
Collected Poems
(1984–2000)

To all those who have persevered for the endurance of humankind.

About the Author

Cecilia Margaret Harding was born in Mansfield, Ohio, U.S.A. and graduated from Case Western Reserve University with a degree in English. She has adventured in numerous areas of the world from game preserves in east Africa, teaching second grade in Managua, Nicaragua to trekking in Nepal. She has attended many universities studying languages and other arts. She ski-raced as an adolescent, studied equitation and ballet. Her photography has been exhibited and she continues to write and study piano in Miami, Florida, U.S.A. where she makes her home.

Contents

Ecdysis[1]

I

Haven't we seen enough of this?
Warblers calling effectlessly to and fro,
Let us carry on the decisions of the round table!
Let us unite and be married.

In mirth we sing, joyfully we bring
Well-hewn stones to ripen
Into berries for our picking
So to peel them gently.

II

Sealing the pact of our cache
We grin and hold the light to our heads
Knowing the satisfaction of our settlement
Is clean and the gavel bound.

Courage grounds our breasts
In a mighty pleated host
Of flames in catapult
To protect the accuracy of our mark.

---

[1] Ecdysis: the act of molting or shedding an outer cuticular layer (as in insects and crustaceans)

III

Kings and Queens we won't
Adjourn as caitiff pirates scouring
Fodder senselessly in sewage
That leaves us hissing.

Here we suborn the demons
To play us hither thither
Irredeemable by the hairless
Wrested, mired, and plagued.

IV

Have you seen the insects?
They were cleeking here yesterday.
Butterflies in yellow, ants in red.
Ladybugs with black dots.

Antennae wandering
Seeking out, seizing
On a sound wave.
We shall see them tomorrow.

V

Blood runs high on our cheeks
As the cold air prickles us
Watching the icebergs melt
Paddling in a chill water.

The sepulcher receives our last hesitation
And the last unknown rite is finally played.
We cannot cheat ourselves
By mixing up the deck.

VI

The rope strengthens
Leading outside the sun
Through stars for navigation
A slumbering realm.

Macaws ready their beaks
To usher in snippeted hippity turtle dandy-hoos.
Cockatoos fulminate a briny roar
As the sharp-billed anchor drops.

VII

Crusty skin is shed.
Let out the roots.
Spread out the world.
Show that the front takes on the life
To give it again in new shades untold.

Raja-poot in cotton 'round a tree
To scale the top by what you see.
Going high, above the sky
Split into branches forming finely.
Little vows exchange helloes.

Bonsai

Missiled reprisals curtail lengthening
Honeysuckle to spin sky-high another way.
Dusty shell powder flies off their backs
Forming dunes to bank upon in later years.

Candle masonry peaking through sand
Against an eye to portend a jewel battening
On secret treasure hordes, garnered and polished,
Chiming in a smooth upward roll.

Propriety

Solid time phases crack new eggs
Inside a wizard's cove of stone tubercles
Bubbling in heat, breathing a closed air
Purified by lustrous endeavor
Of each known moment
Organized to wield discoveries
Reigning sweet bullion for all.

Spheres rise in this volatile blood
Carrying a gem to burst a hundred mysteries,
Evaporating to ether unknown flaws caught at the origin,
Mooring a freshness indomitable
From the start.

Coddle

Shield spun in broadcloth
Warrants a sturdy build
Against rope cutters and blockbusters
Forging a rough way until blade
Knows to sharpen on a strike
An edge turning a point
Towards a wise stock.

Jelly in lemon sprigs form in pools
Between rivulets among grasses
As the course becomes easier
Since truculent pageantry
Finds only a brittle mettle.

On The Bayou

Creole pricks a mix of profuse
And enticing yet fatal glitter in my heart
Which heraldic resistance
Siphons into needlework
Setting all aright
Lest a snipe wreak bitter cane cinder
In canine breakspeed.

Flounce on a taught ride
Carries past canal leg stands.
A finely woven velvet shoe
In bright pattern of arabesque
Clads a toe that taps,
A trumpet rips.
Gay at the knot, dishpans in trail
I move, as an itinerant
Onlooker's ravenous maws
Chew in safety.

Stamp Act

Halvah sudden a thrush
Jumped skyward.
Instead of going down he went up,
Where by the moon, he met a seal.
Together they played for over a day
Until they had had their say
And the moon had none.

Mutiny

A crisp wing breaks on the falling tide
To fan the sand pebbles in panes.
A spider foraging one side, a beetle another,
Burrowing in the unrent robes
Of the tall sandstone sculpture
Of Virgin Mary on the hill
In the neighbor's backyard across the street.

A breeze lifts against these quivering arms,
The stakes of which are unseen,
As the water loosens its grip,
Leaving a pocket full of air
Sliding down the shore.

The Renaissance Room

The rats run among the leaves
Wrestling the keener spent days
As we ran along zigzagged through the trees
By the lagoon.

We didn't go a rowing
But as we looked at Henry IV's saltcellar,
You intimated you would like
To pour liquid from the figure of a breast.

Creaking

Test a stone across the shore,
Sing a beast to sleep upon a cold night.
Stir the lady's widow sense,
Speak the old tones of the new ways.

High snifts the hare across the meadow
Beside the road the bandy-legged
Man hobbles down
In the air that nips.

Autumn Wash

Squirrels scurry across the streets
As we make our way home
In the cold autumn air.
The shingles are loose and as I
Ride along the lake to stop by
And visit a friend, he is busy
Haggling with the woodsman
For a larger cord.

I sit opposite and wonder
Where the cold days go to
Sipping a lager, listening to
His odd English, wishing
He'd called the night before.

The Soil Turns

A ragged terror fills the lonesome veins
In the blue rank room
Of tongues fanning a vacant terminal
Where trains only stop in pits for minutes at a time.

A triumphal arch holds the keystone
Under which parades trumpet melodies
Of victories and saints newly canonized
In the halls of all the popes.

A Belgium Street Sell

On the short upcoming
I raked the streets
Talking to Madame Cassique
Whose son sang at the opera
And unable to make my debut
I cleansed the nuns at the annual street fair.

The old haggard came around there
Seeming to sell old leather craft
And guns to shoot the erring hare
Of a late winter afternoon.

Awash The Sand Alone

Loose flies the night gale
Up the murky blinding gorge
As if I hadn't seen the long shot march
Rounding at the streambed turn.

The sky splinters in streams
And afraid to sleep ashore the sand alone
Lest serpents slither and coil round about my head
I seek the all-remedying panacea of another human.

An Evening

The rest of the crew spun down
The bobsled run. I saw the sleds
Sleighing fast on each run

That ran the whole world down.
If past rhymes held the sea
The waves would hold the heat.

On the sunny afternoon the
Sun's rays hit the pavement and I
Hope charity prevails.

Shaft

The men pass the early evening
Playing go. With or without you,
I will go rolling along.

The old man river goes out
In pain but through that stream
There's something that crawls out of the forest clearing.

Like a light that shines through the branches
Of the trees. The light of the moon
On the seeming edge of darkness.

Attending

At the last, the spears of shuffling Masai
War chiefs ignited the wee sparks
Of night herding castles in the
Parched tufted dusty stomping ground.
Their faces painted and babies hoisted on hips,
The flower remains decorate their faces.

Trap the buffalo so he will feed us,
Pray to the sun which now grows our crops,
So mind not the wind blowing off the Sahara
As the heron fields one last cry
Doomed, whistling on a step.

Making Mount Kenya

The far valleys underfoot
Surge into our view as we near the top.
Our peaked senses scout the marmots
Or other such creatures, pouncing,
Or rushing from the bush.

It's a light drizzle that falls at dusk
As we make our way
Along the streambed meeting walkers
With umbrellas and schoolgirls in white
Blouses and blue skirts
Making McKinder's camp for dinner
And Two Tarn to sleep.

The body has wavered and stammered near the top
To take comfort in a quick camp
Outside of whose tent rises a tripod
Of tall bamboo shoots suspending our food
From the animals.
The comfort of a brother soothes the veins.
At the top we brew our tea and a
Mist rises from the lake
Shrouding our tea-sipping ways
Until we lay our bodies side by side
To brave the night wind hoping our food remains.

The Stove

It was a weary road until
We stopped at your cabin
And the world stopped for a few days
Amid the snow and the forest.

At night the snow crunched under our feet
And the bears must have stood at half bay
While we made our treks out
Amid the stars and fresh air.

The stove hissed as we lay at its feet
Begging its warmth and gave its
Fire heat to ten squirming toes
And two wrestling bodies.

Crossing The Street

The quirky rotund patrolman
Blows his whistle for the children
To cross at the red light.

He blows his whistle at me
If I cross on the other side
When the light is green
And there are no cars coming.

To avoid the little policeman
I cross the street early and
Rush across when there are no cars,
Even when the light is red,
Hoping he won't notice me.

Marketing

The horrid rush at the holiday
To make known the famous assignations
Inflame the heart
And make the wilds tempting.

The hurly-burly of the weekend fest
Points to days viewing art
In an upstate New York art museum
To quell an ancient fist.

Gales

Whither ends the road to peace,
The road along which wars of the soul
Destroy the rose of the flesh?

The steam rises from the rocks in the sauna
And I plunge into the cold water,
Swimming a length to unfurl the tension
Of days gone by.

The winter night is long
And the gusts of wind pierce
The remnants of warmth I have left
To block the blizzard that ravages in time.

The New Rhyme

It was funny, seeing an
Ancient rhyme swell my lips
Seeing that old loves do pass
And the moon brings a new cycle.

I am suckling a new feast
To strengthen my heart
To cherish new moments
And see the tide rise on a sloping bank.

The Hayloft

When you have given the last seconds
Of the crofts airborne, the mice have
Nestled their homes and the snakes
Coil in their dens and instill fear.

It was a leap in the air born of swept,
Purging a festering imbroglio which sent dangling
A body above ground, regardless of fright.
The geography scrupled last minute sight.

Who the wandering the hill passed a
Faery skipping the last fall of
An empire burning at the telescope
Monitoring a cinch to straight.

A red sneaker screamed inside the twine
As the barnyard lurked in the yard
And as the ass stalked and the cocks crowed
We were able to live again.

Fruit Time

The fine rooster sprung on the fence
At the barnyard squabble
As the bay mare jumped across.

The golden cornfields
Spring in the spring.
As cherry blossoms scent
Our air and we take the
Last strains of Mozart
Tickling our exuberance
In an orchard ripe for our picking.

A Rush Of Cold

Signally held at the embrace of one so warm
I cry out hard at the last day
Without human comfort seeking
A warm isle from condemnation.

The dogs rush as I return home,
The geese lift off the water
And I wonder how far I have gone
And how close I am coming
Near a Thanksgiving holiday
From the ones I loved
To the ones I will.

The squeaking, creaking steps of
Someone to announce his austerity
Besides his hands lay my heart out smooth
So I might bear the cold.

Restoration

The north wind routs the senses
As we keel in a small boat
Toward the chilly water
After taking tea at the museum.

You no longer love me as our
Ripened fruit has been peeled all too fast
For the stipend to strengthen our digestion.

Hail me on my way and I will see
You smile a moment long ago
When you pounded the rhythm
Atop a cement slab sculpture
Supported by diagonal strips of metal
On the green near the art school
To my tap scuff clog dance.

The Split

The spendthrift ways that crop
Our felt hats and the ribbons in our hair
Settle on the new faces that proclaim our
Indignity on the front of tiny smiles
Wandering at our incoherence.

The footpaths of our joys make
Insignificant the wrestle of the
Vacuum left between you and me
In the nights of our new separation
From the tired stalks to our cavern
Of respite from the schools of gathering musicians,
And heaving high the arms over
The pliés to a tambourine and entering
The circle on the wrong count to the unkempt byways.

The friends' floors more inviting than
The walk up the hill in high-heeled shoes
After the symphony left
Me knowing I thought too much of myself.

Afoul The Water

When our trembling fingers touch
I wonder how many times a smile
Creeps across your face
And we have known the light of our day.

Wind gusts through our sails
As the sun heightens our glow
From sailing the choppy waters
Of an inland sound.

Yet it is quiet here
And when we are wet from a capsize
The sheen in our hearts
Pounds heavy in our brains.

Midnight Friends

The wind blew off the porch
As our heads bobbed and the sparrows sang
Of our long heralded forages into the night
Which ended the sunny days of summer.

In the dark hours before dawn
We talked at the curbside
Shelling peanuts and waking the suburbs
Of what it would be like to be older.

Nairobi Game Park

The heat hangs heavy in our memories
As the lions play with their cubs
And the wildebeest migrate on the plains.
Outside Nairobi the game park swelters.

I don't want to leave the plains
And I approach a pride of lions at dusk.
Rather than going on, I turn back
And hope not to be luckless in Leopard Gulch.

Nicaragua

We went hunting off
The Nicaraguan Pacific shore.
In Managua, we didn't hear fighting.
The fighting was to the north.

Making our way to school
On the Samosa brick-paved roads
The guards kept their guns
Flat across their stomachs.

Evening

The silent faces that disappear
Into the quiet lodgings at night
See the lights flickering at
Victoria Station in the heavy summer air.

I've a lodging in Gloucester
A little off the main street
And a ways from Buckingham Palace
Where the guards march under tall bear caps.

Pre-Fall Watering

Foreign tongues speak their language
On a rainy summer afternoon
Before the leaves turn and
I've got my place in the world.

The gardens on Martin Luther King Drive
Rest with their headless statuary
And I water the plants in the greenhouse
Hoping to shed some grace.

Bonding

The skulls sit on my doorstep
Waiting to be carried away
By the winds which sneak
Through our doors and windows.

Brace yourself against the frost
That will one day bind
My toes to yours when the peak
Of our senses will fall as the leaves.

Nature

Tiny ships sail in puddles
Around my feet
As the wind curls my ears
And the snow blocks my path
To your door in the hollow.

Make tough fists to fight
The killer bees that may land
On our backs and I will scream
To block their sting.

Alas!

Rain dew spreads on your lips
As I sail my bedroom curtains
Laughing away the mainstream thought
To anchor near a good-hearted cove.

The last days of October
Merit a steady breath
To hold in heat
A stammering smile.

Nocturn

Sing me to sleep
On the whispering trundle bed
Of years prolonged in savory deed
Sifting through owl feathers and rose petals.

The wooden soldiers march around my tearoom
Collaborating with pussy willows,
Which shed their hair on my windowsill
By the turtle dove wooing.

Daylight

Where the autumn trees
Shed their summer coats,
I see your face mustering
My tiny toes to attention.

Finger my soul so I can
See the end of my days
Off some far African plain
In the dusk of a wildebeest trek.

A Round At The Museum

Come upon my heart
To sing a greatness by,
Sing upon my breast to
See the evening's safari fly.

Greet me in the morning,
Sing my breast to rise,
Swear upon my soul
To give all I care.

East Wing

Swiping a street fed heart,
West, to see the woman's baby cart,
Which the Buddha snapped.
Twelve fierce men march down the avenue
Singing "Stop War" and I
Shall sing a lullaby.

Bring me a watermelon
To set on the table
Where each new eagle
Sweeps a canyon sky.

Crest

The water rests on my lips
As I taste the new morning dew.
Sift the golden leaves
Under the wooden church pew.

Melt the tiny pine ships
That sail my stormy seas .
Teach the old wind
To loosen its grip upon my wobbly knees.

The Rise Of Autumn

Red apples fall on the land
Off the northern coast
Where the water laps the sand
And my virginity beckons the most.

An old terrier barks at the music
Upon the marble floors
Where the miner seizes his pick
And the fog spreads over the moors.

The Ticking Of Wax

The point of my needle weaves in and out
To stitch a dream on cloth
Where my head touches without doubt
Lanterns of light circled by a moth.

The leaves stick to the windows
As I court the silver candlestick
Topped by wax floes
The dripping of which beats the clock tick.

Leaves Dropping

The June bugs have all hidden for the season
Masking their antennae in some stuffed place
To surprise us all in their reason
At not showing up until their period of grace.

Sing the praises of Solomon
To my frisky ears
When silence reduces fun
To a tiny trickling of tears.

The moon shudders on the rise
To a song of the old time
When angels sang in white cloth guise
And the sea coughed up lime.

Fancy my skirt blowing in the bitter night
To the raccoons who take fright
At the running light
When all is out of sight.

A Season's Tale

The spring seems a long season off
As winter creeps up our sleeves and over
Our faces scourging the homeless
And haunting the trash can scavengers.

The whisper of a child in my ear
Sends the small fine hairs
Crawling at lightning pace
In a small room before Christmas.

Encouragement

I have company again
So the nights aren't so painful
And all the places I've been
Don't seem to take so high a toll.

The freezing air stirs my child sense
And the little wonder I have left remains
To the childhood days whence
The bear and the crocodile sang many refrains.

The busy street makes me shudder
At any human being left alone
To face a shorter hour
Walking singly prone.

Touch the years I have left
With your funny smile
And I will bridge the cleft
Left by a frightful while.

Snow

The beat of your heart
Sets my ticking apart
To the stars at the start
Where mistletoe sprigs taste tart.

Father Christmas, give me your tiding
At the onset of snow hiding
To the blustery wind pushing
My only song to you biding.

Chill

The dripping of the rain
Rests on my coat in the autumn air
And I listen to the strain
Of a wind chilling the colorful fair.

Whistle a sacred tune
To wrestle the shortening days
When the leaves shed soon
And old folks part their ways.

On The Way To Greece

The night hour bears down hard
When the chimpanzees swallow
To ponder a dreadful shard
As Kikuyu in the forest follow.

Send me at arm's length
To your fortress basking
In an Acropolean sea
Where turtles lay eggs for our sucking.

The Tearoom

The weary ones snuggle deep below
As the sparrows sing a duet
And the caterpillars scoot along the road.
I will go now to my fellow's house.

The sacred ones make their way to the river
As mother calls, "Tea is served".
Have a round with me
And I shall sing thee praises.

Towards an evening bed
The air of frost stirs 'round my bones.
Wait a minute
To hear the creaking of a neighbor's steps.

Geneva

Marchionesses play on my windowsill
As the wind rattles
The buttresses to my fortress
In the room where I sleep at night.

The song lingers in my ears
To the step of bouncing tubas
And rumbas directed
By the man in white gloves and red and blue
Uniform with brass buttons
Walking backwards, proceeding down the street.

Into The Village

They all marched down the street
That day, with horns blowing and
Drums beating. They played a song
That all the Swiss knew and stopped
Before me and the rest of the
People walking in the street,
Who stopped too.

Fountains sprung from Lake Geneva
And I had just walked down from
My palatial summer residence where the
Count of Palermo lived, to buy a pair of sunglasses.
They were tortoiseshell and standing
In the sun that fall day with the
Water running close by, I felt I
Could end my days in that city.

Token

Take my picture when the
Sun has gone down and
I am sipping tea near a fire
At the day's edge of gladness.

Paint my face when the sunlight ceases
And the darkness is just a little ways off
So I'll clear the space
Left at that juncture.

Carve my body in wood so that
On a bright day you'll have a figure
To hold you by until
The light ceases and no more shadows play.

Sculpt my head in clay
So that before the casting
I'll have a chance to fix a hair or two
And you'll have a bronze bust.

It's coming on winter
And I just want you to
Have something left of me
Before I go.

Time

Gather the leaves that surround your head,
Hold the feathers close in your hands,
Sift the sawdust from between your fingers,
Touch the fur 'round your feet.

The sparrow sings in my head.
The turtle lays eggs for me to collect
On the sand at midnight.
Sprinkle marjoram on lemon.

O you magician,
Transform me into something real
And bless my eternal being.

Born To Walk

He was born to walk alone
The sorrowful stones until
The pheasants flew toward
The sky when junipers spread
Toward the heavens.

The circle closes me in you
And the squire takes forth the joy
As women weep in halls
Taking a last call.

Sing, O the wise ones!
Sing of the hills, of the maidens, of the shepherds!
Sing of the flower blooming in the springtime!
Guard, O angels of paradise!

Before A Time

Oh! The chants of rhyme
Swing in my bosom
A crusty chime
To end all my days by the shore.

But I know you have not seen me yet
Swooping in the days of the long past
Where swallows lift off St. Francis
And he holds his hands to the sun.

Bear the new fruit that betokens
Your gentleness in myriad stays
Beneath a cloth pining to sail
Full across the roaring ocean.

Preach not a song I've had on my lips
The days trailing behind your soft shoe
Shuffle, so I won't linger in the
Streets anymore 'til dinnertime.

Cast off the haircloth shirt
Swaying in the breeze like a mammoth
Searching out her young midst
A storm-drenched valley.

Singers

Wrestle a bear tooth
To spin a very fine web
Through your mouth to mine,
When whispers carry you through.

Spread open your fingers
And spoon-feed the baby sparrows
Nestling near the tree
Far from you and me.

Sell the autumn wind
That has held some respite today,
In the billows that have swept here recently,
To bring in a flagging hand.

Solace

Scratch the dust from off this book
So that I might have one last look
Before you leave to go to sea
And we might be left alone, just you and me.

Spread those fingers wide
So that I might not hide
Between the covers at dawn
And blow these pages across the lawn.

O seafarer, stay with me awhile
And I will cross with you a fair stile
That separates these two fields
And we will see what time wields.

The music rushes through my ears
And I think of you these years
When the touch of your hand
Stands my soul on end like a marching band.

Remembrance

Sip this tea gently
And smile intermittently,
As we take this time
To watch ourselves grow.

Slip into your coat
As we might watch the sailboats on the sound
For the last time
Making their way to land.

Let us go skating in winter
And glide over the ice,
Two by two
As we make smoke of the cold out our mouths.

A Wedding Song

I

I to thee wed.
To you I unite in spirit
All my joys and secrets.

Take my sadness
And weave castles in my sand dunes.
Take my hands around your waist.

Send my love across the way,
Send me kisses on the wind.
Spray my love with yours.
Tickle my insides pink and make sure
I go down slow among the leaves this fall,
And give my love to the children,
When all has startled a herald's cove.

II

Tackle a major incline
To tame a blossom to calm a storm,
When a snowy blizzard
Rises to the helm.
Sing to the sun a rhyme,
To sport wings on a chariot
Rich with holidays
By fires in lodges
To kindle my flame
At each moment.

Wander carefully through my mind,
And sing a jubilant tune in my ears.

Make sure the chimes take the
Morning news into the loved ones' feet.

Sweet morsel,
Know that you are mine.
Belt out the sacred canons
Far and wide.

To those who will listen.

III

Mark my words that come in
Off the branches of trees,
In the midwinter to catch us all
At the maypole
Celebrating the ruins of Greece
In a sunset going out at sea.

Sack my horrors and take my wild temper
To the jubilant streets below
In the nakedness of my spirit.
Bring the tip of the sapling
Growing strong into your hands,
To project you to the next
Coming off with a simple spring.
Suck my nectar and refill my veins,
With sweeter wine
To make an end to my days.

So, let the day begin fresh.

IV

And to think we've reached heaven today
By the miracle of God,
To be proclaimed by all
Under one
To hope for the meadows of spring.

Now that heaven reigns in this world
Let us rejoice and make fun.

Glory to God in the highest
To cover my back with your arms.
Sing a lullaby
And I will swim on a sunny day.

V

On the wings of Saturn
You and I will fly
To unknown places
Across the sky.
To Siberia and the Sahara,
Where all is cold and dry
And the hot and cold rise off the plains.

This train will soon go away
Off the cold winter ground, when the
Night's clay turns malleable
Upon a day where the steam blows out our mouths.

Call to the heron before it flies.

VI

Bear this tiding in all hallowedness
So the wreaths on our doors
Betoken our mirth
And the red blood fares high on our cheeks.

Sing to the meadows and pastures
Of days to come,
When the robins will be outside our gardens
And the bears in the wood out from hibernation.

Oh! I thee wed in the plenitude
Of our happiness and thus we shall
Bring mirth in rounds,
Upon our family and friends.

VII

You spill beauty into me
As I make my rounds each day
And nod asleep in your arms.

I thee wed.

Notice my smiles are a lot broader
As I make my life with you,
As if walking by a stream
In midsummer fields.

Take this vow
And make it yours
For all time.

Thinking Of Spring

The water is almost ice now
And we have passed a few snowy days together,
Rambling outside with our hoods over our heads
Nestling as soon as we find a warm place.

The starlings sing outside our window
And we will see birds soon enough,
To break the winter spell
Into fresh blossoms for our smelling.

The Night Long

So the sparrows have all gone south
For the winter, leaving you and me
To see the cold winds together
And sip tea quietly,
On this ground for you and me.

We shall see the Southern Cross again,
Before the winter winds have
Done too much harm
To our souls lurking in this northern clime.

Wrest the strings of my warm heart,
Humming for your touch.
Fingers that run my back long,
In the heat between you and me.

Be Merry

Sweet fingers touch my sheets
As the pigeons walk along the railroad tracks
By the transit station,
And we make our way down the hill
And file through the passageway.

It is Christmas time
And we give gifts.
So sing chimes of old
And press your lips to mine upon this snowy evening.

Christmas

As Christmas nears
The snow gathers on the ground
And ice covers the road.

The birds' nests are empty
But these feathered friends
Will return in the spring.

Sing the hails of yesterday
To bring the new ones to bear.

Holy Times

July seems a far way from December
But this cold day sends a million signals
Down my spine to burrow neatly
In my soul during the
Time when Christ was born.

I don't go to church
But I would like to pray sometime,
When Christ is risen at Easter
And we have seen the many
Shrouds all over Europe.

Blessed

Dear good ones, take this well,
To know that charity has prevailed
In springtime when flowers are in full bloom,
And water streams from the mountain sides.

Peace is given to ones who nestle
And bring a babe into the world
To swathe and coddle and coo
When the minstrel plays tunes.

Holiday

Swing high the Christmas wreath,
Nail up the mistletoe
And hook the ornament
So to admire the Christmas joy.

Hark the herald angels sing.
Let us free our arms and legs
To the calling of the grouse
On the heather.

A Christmas Carol

The traveling young men in their overcoats
Fill Grand Central Station at this time,
To run home to their loved ones and families.
Christmas Eve is here.

Brothers and sisters
Gather around the tree and sing,
And laugh and comfort
Before the day of the big feast.

Kaplan's Drawing Room

Hear the songs at Christmas past,
These days where I've been singing,
These months past,
Humming across the snow
And whistling into pine cones.

We visited and merried
Amongst friends and danced
And drank with champagne glasses
As the father pranced
In Viennese knickers,
Afghanistani vest,
Executive Santa Claus tie,
And YSL white shirt,
Pointing to Warren G. Harding's
Square grand piano.

We laughed and listened to
Our childhood recitals
And took to the warmth of the fire.

A Snowy Afternoon

The snow piles up outside my window
This winter, as I sing and smile,
As frost gathers on the panes
And the neighbors shovel the sidewalks.

It gets dark early now and I am left
With you to share my secrets
And fears about myself and the world
Where people get shot walking down the street.

I will try and forge some niche
And allow room for you,
As my nest piles up inside my window
And I make do with books, papers and pens.

Bright Geneva

I lived outside Geneva
In the hills where we could look
Down upon the lake
And where we would hike
Above the berry farms.

It was a move from a summer villa
Inside the old city above the university.
The wind swept the leaves inside
The walls of the school courtyard
Inside of whose halls literature lectures
Spun off the tongues of scholars.
I sat amazed.

Every Saturday I would go
Outside the city
For a riding lesson
At an English stable
On a horse named Ioba.

Respite

The frost has receded
This fine winter's eve
As I lie nestled in this attic
On the third floor
In East Cleveland.

Friends become married
And friends call
At the wee hours
Until our hearts give
And we go to bed.

Hearts

Once the bell chimes
The cold ones huddle in houses
That keep out the wind
That blows from Canada over the lake.

The shingles plaster down the roofs
And the house is warm,
Keeping little babies' hearts pounding
And the grown-ups from sneezing.

The cat purrs at the fireside
And mice are far away,
While we stitch our clothes
Waiting for the next card game.

Waiting For Spring

The winter thaw is welcome,
But the snow from Alaska sounds
Foreboding as we must look
For a new house soon.
It is February and
I can hardly wait for spring.

The trains rumble through
This neighborhood on schedule,
And I hope the spring
Will warm my veins again
As the birds begin to sing
And the plants and trees blossom.

Watching The Ocean

The crocus spring from the soil
And with a garden I might toil,
When the days are long
And the sun beats down strong.

Oh summer muse, take these wings
And make them free also,
So that I might sail to Innisfree
On a long glide northeast.

Take the plea that is mine
So that I might cast a spell,
And not float too far out seaward
On the Atlantic side
Of Nicaragua in a hazy morning
As I sit watching the ocean,
Propped up on the sand
By a large piece of driftwood.

Every Living Day

Dear Sirs, I have forsaken
The foes of my past,
And learned to love new ones
Where God shines on this good earth.

Bless the simple, so they shall love
And be loved as the warmth
Of the sun shines on the
Archeologists and anthropologists
And anarchists as the rainbow
Spreads overhead.

I have loved and will love
Every living day,
Until the halo of my sphere
Rises into the ether of eternity.

Take my sums and they will be yours
On a good Tuesday afternoon,
As it is summer and it has
Rained on our shorts as we
Have walked through the Italian neighborhood
To a concert at the music school.

Sing Praises Of Solomon

As the sun sets on the ocean
The tennis matches lurch in my mind,
Thinking of matters that could be,
Dreaming of carriages
Trimmed with flowers.

Once is not enough
As the blood flows through these veins
Walking in girlhood fields,
Through manly estates
To see a moment's pride.

But alas! The fields are no more
And I see the castaway invitation
To the hunt.
So therefore I am listless
At the art museum,
Yet happy to know
There are two Rome prizes.

Let a baby's heart sing
To a frisky environment.

Dusk In Nairobi

The stars have fallen
And the beasts have settled
On the African plains,
As vultures fly in close
And I ride past their carrion.

The sun beats down hard
On the old Kabeti Road,
Up which old men push their carts,
And the sun sets strong
In a suburb outside Nairobi.

The natives sing at the end of the day
To the blaze of crackling fires.
Their voices drift into the house
And the night watchman
Outside my window
In his long coat and cap
Makes tapping on the gravel.

The children pack so tightly
On the bus I fear pickpockets
And am relieved when
We reach the drive of our home.

Bearing Offspring

Hail the mother that brought me here
As I enter mid-adult life,
Cooking every evening at home
And knitting after dinner.

She is now a good friend
Whom I miss dearly and
Think of when I am alone,
Walking down a city sidewalk.

It was she who first set
Me upon a horse and led
Me in the snow on a sleigh.

I miss the hayrides.

Summer On Nigh

The gardens in Boston bloom
And sailboats whiz on the Charles River.
I miss you in the day
And love to be with you at night.

My baby pillows lie on your big pillow
And I busy myself
With needlepoint and knitting
Until you come home in the evening.

Tonight we will go to the planetarium.
I have forgotten my Nietzsche
And Freud to gardening
By loosening the earth and planting seeds.

Set Atwitter

The dancer watched with
The washerwoman as the line
Of masters candidates walked by,
And I applauded heartily
As my very own friend's
Name was called.

We could not endure
The woman who had been in
Prison and tortured in China
As the guest speaker of commencement,
So we went and had eggs nearby
And talked about children.

On An Eve

O through this slumbering realm
I will creep with unmitigated step
To lands in heaven where sheep graze
And all the traffic of my mind settles.

Raise the light step of children
And their soft cheeks I will kiss
When the sun lowers and the sharecroppers
Have finished their day.

Passing Into Fall

Summer is gone and fall
Brings on cold nights,
So we will sit by the fire
And reminisce the warm days.

Remember our life that is
Ripening with the seasons,
And we will sing to the children
Who pass us skipping.

A Summer Day

Mice run freely on the farm
As I paddle on the river
And my head brushes on the willow branches.
The water rats shinny upon the waves,
Reaching land, upon which they shake
Their coats.

Flying squirrels flutter through
The trees and I shell peanuts on the shore.
The crabs scuttle over the sand
And I hope to find a pearl
In a gaping mollusk.

Entering Church

Immediately as we entered the pew,
My mother knelt and prayed.
The four of us lingered, hoisting
Ourselves up onto the seat,
Settling in to listen to the minister.

I didn't understand any of his words
And liked to sing from the books
And liked it even more when the
Organist started up that very special refrain
That signaled us to wriggle out of
The pew and cross in front of the
Congregation under the pulpits and on
To Sunday school.

I thought maybe if I kneeled
On the prie-dieu as my mother did
I might talk to God too,

Closing my eyes
And resting my head on crossed arms
Like my mother
On the pew back.

Breathing

It was unnerving
To see the winter last so long
And the waterfowl sullied so,
But maybe there is light again
Creeping up from the receding shadows
To play on our faces
While we endeavor to stop
The impending disaster.

Do not stand mute to greed
And destruction, war and famine,
Or the pollution of our earth,
Which sustains our smiles, our hugs,
Our signaling, and those forays
Into art and experimentation
Which enable us to breathe.

Walking In Asia

As dawn broke in the Himalayas,
The Sherpas set tea inside
Our tents and we would bustle to
Our senses to face the new snow outside.

We trekked up that valley
For what seemed like ages,
Passing monasteries, rhododendron groves,
Yak herders, welcome posts and teahouses.

At one of our last camps
We spread our sleeping bags out in
A small wooden lean-to.
After dinner we danced with
The Nepalis, facing out to the fire,
Arms linked in arms, shuffling forward,
Kicking out one leg and then the other.

The next night, we drank beer in the
Rickety teahouse just down the path,
At a table next to twenty
Lice-ridden beds for other trekkers.

Our final walk to the end
Of the valley lifted our spirits,
For there was little snow left and the sun
Shone brightly on the green grass.

We sang to the moon those last
Evenings amid the peaks
And scaling an icefall as a
Storm moved in reawoke our
Frail solitary stance in an environment
Over which we had little control.

Coming down the mountain that spring
Children ran barefoot on the paths,
Among the grasses and the wild flowers
Like newborn colts frolicking,
Kicking, bucking and nipping
At each other's tails.
My smile was more exuberant as I
Met walkers, some bent over under a
Heavy weight of sticks for burning,
Or some other cargo, knowing I would
Soon reach the bottom.

In The Wilderness With Demons

We were walking from the wee
Hours at dawn, to dusk, at the
Heels of a half-crazed former French
Alpe guide, who upon seeing a verdant
Mountain slope, would seize the occasion
To climb it at once, expecting us
Weary ones to follow in
The same inspired step.

He led us over a crumbling ridge
Down whose sides fell rocks and stones
From the pressure of our feeble steps.
In front of me, my tentmate was crying,
Yet as we sat in camp outside our tent
That night she cradled our other tentmate
In her lap and sang nursery songs.

As we lay in our sleeping bags
A great swishing occurred outside in
The tall grass, and although I
Knew it must have been a herd of deer
Passing through, my lesser instinct
Convinced me whatever it was was going to
Devour us, upon which
I jumped into the closest sleeping bag.

Thinking they had passed after a rather
Long period, I climbed back into my own.

In the morning, a few yards from our tent,
The tall grass was matted down
In an area of about thirty feet 'round.

The monsters had been there quite awhile.

A Summer Night With Horses

We rode out under the stars
One starry Ohio night, through
The woods, along the stream,
To an open field where we made camp.

The embers glowed in the fire
Around which we lay in sleeping bags,
And I, only ten, nestled up against
The ranch-owner's son.

My mother had ridden her horse,
And my brother rode a large pony.
That summer the same pony got caught
On a barbed fence he was trying
To get over, and in the fall I took
His skull to school for show and tell.

The fire sputtered its last breath
And we slept. As dawn broke
We awoke to find the horses
Had escaped from their ties and roamed,
So, as we ate our breakfast,
The ranch hands scouted them out.

Children In The Attic

We entertained the reporters and photographers
By opening up a crate
Of stuffed Winnie-the-Pooh characters from
My mother's college days,
Each of which she would buy
After passing an exam.

Delving into the costumes stored
For the community theater,
We donned old dresses, hats and
Robes with braided belts of an obese opera singer.

I was not captured singing an aria,
But putting on lipstick in a
Cotton jumper with curly gauze
Around the arm openings, and saying vainly,
"I hope no one at the garden party
Has a dress like mine".

My brother sat in a box wearing
A longhaired wig with a pirate's hat,
Grinning ecstatically.
The reporters said he was sailing his
Ship on the high seas.

Another brother stood, not knowing quite how to react,
Staring intently, in a long-sleeved
White shirt the tails and cuffs of which
Barely touched the floor around
His tiny saddle shoes.

The little neighbor friend I brought
With me, for her picture, sat cross-legged,
Wearing a shawl and tilting a parasol
Over her shoulder, and curling back her lips
Proclaimed, "The cheesecake is marvelous".

The Lost Kingdom

We swept furiously the floor
Of a pine grove that Saturday afternoon,
The neighborhood children and I,
Hoping to establish the seat of our kingdom.

No one meted out the different tasks
Assuming the role of monarch or ruler,
We each knew instinctively what
Merited attention, and applied ourselves forthwith.

From our royal seat, not only the
Neighborhood, but all the land would be ours,
We would play and gambol all the daylong
Retaining order through noble deeds.

No one knew what the distribution
Of power among us would be
But we tidied the sanctuary fiercely, never
To go to school again, or go home again,
Until our respective bells rang for dinner
And the pace slowed, some lingering on principle.

A Ceremony

The bowling lawns glistened
With dew under the morning sun,
Behind the old white house
Awaiting a ceremony to unfold.

At first, the hair fell in long locks
From the scissors and my glee,
And then they cut near my head,
One blade crossing the other,
Not producing so much substance,
But pulling enough to give the
Scalp a sweet tingling.

It felt so good, I urged the
Cutter to continue, beyond the normal,
Acceptable short length. She pioneered
And I enjoyed the sensation of tiny pins
Grazing my head.

It was not elegant, or even in vogue,
But somehow signified a cleansing of
The old ways, and a new beginning.

Swimming Apart

I made little noises to fill
The gap of the silence between you and me.
We swam lengths
In the pool without even so
Much as smiling at each other.

The sounds of feet and arms splashing
In the water reverberated off the walls,
And we would occasionally stand
In the shallow end peeping out
From under goggles, resting our
Hands on our hips.

The water slid over my body
As I journeyed to the deep end,
In breaststroke, my arms gliding
And fanning, my legs giving
Frog kicks.

Diving to the bottom of the deep end
To investigate a black brick,
My head almost exploded from
The pressure and I
Quickly rose to the top.

For His Own Sake

He lifted the mouse out of the cage
By its tail and stroked it for
A few seconds.
Then he set it on my thigh,
And it scrambled a few paces.

As I remember, I would pass
Into either of my brothers'
Rooms where mice ran all night on
Wheels in cages, which emitted the
Smells of woodchips.

They barely let me squeeze next to them
But let the mice crawl all over
Their necks and shoulders.
When they began to count the newborn
Mice in the bathtub in twenty-five
Cent increments, my mother decided
To give up breeding because the
Little boys no longer valued them
For their own sake.

David At A Tea Party

There was a roller coaster in
Our backyard over whose hills and dales
My older brother would ride in
A little car until it reached the end,
And leveled out.

Later, he asked me to help him
Transport an octagonal Chinese table
Of his girlfriend's and we set it
On an oriental rug in a field
Next to a cow pasture and sat
In low wooden children's chairs
Sipping whiskey out of small porcelain
Teacups while someone exercised
Their horse at a distance
In a canter around us.

Towing The Line

It was a gray Ohio afternoon
And my mother pulled my brother and me
On a wooden sled along the road past
The woods to Nana and Grandaddy's house.

Snow was everywhere, on the trees,
On the road, the roofs, creaking
Under my mother's steps and the
Runners of the sled.

The sun came out as we passed
The pony stable and the crack
Of branches in the woods
Echoed long afterwards.

Evading Nursery School

The boulevard had grassy islands
In the middle and every morning,
I would ascend wooden steps and
Enter a rather dark house, passing
Through the living room,
The dining room, and descend
Into the basement.
I only remember the toy house
Appliances under the steps and
The bookcases on the walls.

I played house a few times
And when I staged a protest,
Declaring I was no longer coming,
Mrs. Torrence allowed me to choose
A couple of books to take away.
One was *The Night Before Christmas*
And the other was about a possum
Who had lost and then found
Its splendid red coat.

People would wait weeks to
Be able to clap the cymbals
As the leader of the parade
In which we marched up the basement steps,
Playing all sorts of instruments,
Snaking through the living room,
Into the dining room, around the table,
Back into the living room,
And down the steps.

I played the cymbals once or twice
But the day I took the books
Away, I never came back.

A Morning With Elizabeth

I knew it was getting late,
Maybe around nine o'clock,
But being in my grandparents' guest room,
Under the silken covers,
I didn't want to get up.

Elizabeth came into the room
And lay down beside me on the bed.
She said I might want to think
About getting up, and I said Okay.
We lay there for a few minutes
Together on the bed.

I got dressed and went down to
The breakfast table, adjacent the kitchen.
Sitting at the head of the table, I looked
Out the big window past the melons
Ripening on the sill, to the trees and flowers.
She brought me cereal covered with strawberries.

The Charms At San Xavier Del Bac

The sun was rising, barely, and
We made our way out to the
Mission a few miles out of town.
We took pictures of each other
Standing in front of the entrance.

I walked up the hill following you.
Your sandal kept slipping off
Into the dust powder of the path.
We looked out on the land from
A balustrade and then walked
To the shrine.

There was a cast iron fence all around
And charms of ribbons
And Christmas ornaments tied to
The intersection of a horizontal rod,
Running near the top.

We talked about the charms
On the way down,
Taking single frame sequence shots
Of each other walking very gingerly,
Arms stretched out, balancing
Across a row of rocks,
The projected movement on the screen
Being funny, showing us in
Different positions in our trajectory.

The Pixiecrat

There is a little light
In the room
Coming from the window.

He stands three feet high
And a bow from his robe
Around his waist
Is on his stomach.
The tips of his ears are pointed.
Hair swirls on his head.

The twinkling of his eyes
Indicates the platform
Of the minutiae.

After Dinner

I was sitting on the floor and
Gazing at everyone's feet and calves,
When my mother urged me to
Gain Nana's feet stealthily,
And tickle until she peed.

It was great fun yet our end
Was not achieved. Our intent was
Not entirely serious.
I must have wandered over to
The big leather armchair and
Spread out across Grandad's knees
When the ruckus died down
To have my back rubbed.

It wasn't clear to me
What the adults were saying,
But I knew the evening
Was winding down and soon enough
We were out the door
On the walk waving good-by.

At The Theater

In the movie Vincent van Gogh
Cut off his ear
And when he finally died,
By shooting three bullets into his side,
He was lucky:
His family and friends mourned in state.

The men wore top hats that
Had black veils hanging down the back.
When his brother separated
From the crowd accompanying the casket
To the graveyard into the field
Of yellow sunflowers,
Raging at the injustice of Vincent's
Death, I admired his mid-calf
Black coat, remembering how hard
I tried to procure one from a
Costume proprietor, having carried
Bag after bag of costumes to winter storage.

For one of his coats the Smithsonian
Made him one, to his specifications.

Maybe I should have taken a long
Black mid-calf coat the first night
I tried on several others.

Visitors In The Country

We pounded on the keys
In the music room one
Blustery winter afternoon
And out the door of the house
Tore down the hill
Wrapped in mufflers,
Heaving.

Heaving hi heaving ho
We reached the lunchroom.
I didn't understand why
They sat across from me so proudly
But knew he had her golden flute.

I retaliated by pitying them
Only to be unprepared,
Left without friendship,
Floundering.

I asked after the golden flute
From time to time.
He finally sent it back to her.

Calliopi

I

Our ears are red from muffling
Over the ever-changing ice floes,
Our heads rise and we tilt our faces
Skywards to welcome the dawn.

Sweep clear the atmosphere
To whisk off the impure dust,
Approaching us in a
Turbulent untimely fury.

II

The primordial rustlings
Loose their tendrils
To reach us walking
On the land.

Hi ho clean shall we know our day
Touching each essence,
Turning our souls
Into a chalice whose nectar
Prospers forever afterwards.

III

How the toadstools burgeon!
Stop the poisons from spreading
Into fungi, which rattles
Against this seepage annihilating atoms.

If we summon the worst
Of the mites crimson wreaths
Will continue to whistle a flag
To pull at our shoes.

IV

Cast off the coats and the shackles
Binding our hands and feet,
So that we may enter
Our gains at the start.

Tidings to the brave waters
Carrying our forthrightness
Spiraling out from the shouts
Of our hearts.

A Few Small Places Above Geneva

As I walked up the hill
On the road, I saw a man
Whom I first saw
When arriving in this town,
Delivering eggs to the woman
Who let me stay in her house.

He was high on a horse-drawn wagon
Beside his daughter; behind them
Was a mound of hay.

This afternoon he was kneeling
Planting a tree as I passed
And nodded to him.
The drizzle was letting up.

I walked past his farm on a path
Curving next a field of cows
In the woods to a tiny hamlet.
A woman who had resided there
A long time came out
Wearing wooden clogs.
There was a well there. We paused
And I continued walking.

I supped in the eating house
Across from my dwelling
With migrant construction workers
From France and when I saw the man
Who was planting the tree float
Inside holding high a tiny present
Wrapped with a pretty bow in the air

Like a plane and sit with his son
And the Count of Palermo, and his friend,
There was much cause for celebration.

We sang between tables
One parrying the other
Heedless of the waiter and cook,
Until I rose, gave a final
Nod to the fête,
And bid all adieu.

The Dickson Estate

I looked across from my house
To the field where Mr. Perry
Was mowing on a tractor
Down from the house.
With my brother and friends
We ran to greet him.
He invited us up and we rode
On his lap and fenders.

David and I explored the totem pole,
Rising across from the stable
In front of and to the side
Of the rose garden.

At this time when the grass grew tall
Around the cast iron seat for two,
Inside and throughout the garden,
The skeleton keys landed in his hands.
He went all the way in.
I trailed through a few doors.
As he went into the drawing room
I stayed outside peeping through the keyhole.

He appeared by a black grand piano
Small as he was, on a red rug
Surrounded by red velvet curtains
Festooning the windows.
I hoped he would hurry back.
There were some moments
When I didn't see him.

Later, when the fields were no more,
Or the orchards,
Or the garden,
Or the stable,
Or the totem pole,
Or the house,

After the land was parceled out
For smaller dwellings,
I sat by the curb one day
The sun bearing down through the clouds
On the edge of where the fields were
And a small black and white mutt
Appeared dappled like the cows I saw
In the picture of Mousehead Heath,
After looking at one of Durham Cathedral.

Nosferatu

He appears through the centuries
Without white gloves before the nets
On the ships floating on the rivers,
On the locks, in the oceans and in the canals.
As he arrives amidst the crates teeming
With rats, he ponders to go over land
In a phaeton on the roads by the bluffs
Or on top of the cars in the trains on the tracks.
Maybe he will come to our party tonight
Or peer in on the ball to dance.
Maybe he will strike a note on the three-tiered
Lightly strung wind chime.
Maybe he will light the candles on our table.
His ears are pointed as they rise to a distinct tip
Orienting his next decision to raise the masts
On a schooner to weave through the islands
In the Beaufort Sea, or to set the sails on a galleon,
Towering as the figurehead at the bow
Towards the Societies or to adjust the buttons
On the control panel of a submerged vessel
To glide towards the Spice Islands and on to Borneo.
Or to stand above the weir in the clearing
As the mist rises.
He shall see us as we shall see him.

Coming Up

The flowers came up this spring
Like tiny parasols on men's top hats,
Shading my dismay with tints of yellow
And white and red and orange.

The flowers laced my happiness
With delicate traces of bubbling,
After a dark gloomy season when
The sun shone little and nary
A bird sang at my window.

Pugsley In The Tropics

He stepped off the airboat
Walked through the tall grass
And into the mango grove.
Purple green and pink were
The colors of the fruit
Some of which he pulled
Back the skin and sunk his teeth
Into the ripe meat, some of which
He ate the skin alone.
The lizards arrived in fifty crates
Which he stacked in rows
One upon the other
For his next experiment.

Humid Air Rising

I dared not cross the fields
Full of cows lest a bull be amongst them.
How fast might I have run,
If I dared cross their field.

The ground was fuzzy with life
Surviving on what I trod underfoot.
Not far off the fresh cut hay
Sprinkled the fields in cylinders.
A lone tree in the middle broke the yellow expanse.

A Hobo By Chance

Amid the voluptuous curves of
The rambling estates sat a hobo
On a three-legged stool
Eating his lunch by a stream,
Whose discovery provided a delightful surprise.

We were three and such
A spectacle was so enchanting,
We stood awhile in awe of
Something so different,
Making it our secret,
Revealing it to no one.

Poised For An Hour Or So

The green wool carpet sank
Sensuously an inch under each step
As I climbed the grand stairway
From the entrance hall to the waiting room
For the musicians on the story above.

We sat collected, the sun shining
Through the tall windows, waiting our turn.

The piano was different from the
One at home, lighter to the touch.
I played my ten pieces effortlessly.
The judge was quite amiable,
Exchanging smiles with me.
His grades were mostly favorable
And I walked out of the stone mansion
Holding the certificate with the grades
Showing I passed into the bright
Summer day anticipating my
Swift and vigorous bicycle ride
Into the country.

Country Air

In the lane between the yard
And the hayfields, I sat perched
High up on the branch of a tree
Surveying as far as my eye might
Reach in the moonlight and clear
Sky one summer's eve at midnight.

The cricket's choir at its peak,
The barely discernible form of the cows
In the far-off fields, we barely
Exchanged a word, my overnight guest and I,
She in the next tree, as my parents
Slept sound in their bed,
Without a trace of our absence.

For awhile I was petrified,
Even up in the tree, quiet, attracting
No attention, until the dawn came,
Relieving my terror as if its light
Insured my unadulterated safety.

A Simple Time

It was just a funny little day,
The air crisp, around the beginning of school,
And being just a funny little girl,
And the weekend, I decided to ask
The little girl a few houses down
If she would have a late lunch with me
In the median between her house and the next.

With my tin red and black plaid pail
I arrived and we arranged ourselves
On the grass, beginning our repast
Without ceremony.
It was just before the leaves fell
And the scent of apples fallen from
Their trees permeated the air.

A Heart Letting Loose

We have won an hour or so.
The light playing with our shadows
On our fronts reveals curious images
As we pass from the village
To the mountains.

From the shore
We call for more.

O timid birds twittering
In the bush,
Fly out across the gorge.
Upwards soar.

In the ray of light
Specks of matter mingle.

We walk and make camp before sunset.
In the dark a fire burns,
Around which faces sparkle
With twinkling eyes and glistening teeth.

Figures Of A Voyage

I divined the beggar
In an undefined shape
Wrapped in coarse cloth
Sleeping on the steps
In front of the market hall.

Out on the plains
Wildebeest and zebra
Walked in single file, migrating.

The air was pregnant
With a journey that had not yet begun.

Mustering A Decision

The snow was melting
On the mountains and I sat
Gazing at them in the barnyard.

That winter we shoveled snow
Off the roof of one barn,
Furiously, from fear of it
Crushing in the roof.

I had no insight or hindsight
On my situation, only knowing
How wonderful was the rippling blue sky,
And the black birds flying high overhead,
The new calves in the pastures, the sprouting
Green of the fields,
The coyotes howling on the neighboring
Hills at night.

Maybe, only if I had accepted
My situation, and been brave enough
To forge on, would my course
Have been different.

Upon Entering And Leaving A Village

The Nepali children were happy
As they stood on porches in front of
Houses, and inside windows, gazing,
Smiling, and scrutinizing us as we
Entered their villages, graciously
Assembling for a photograph.

Their hair standing every which way,
Their faces dirty, they persisted
In their inquisitiveness and
Scampered around us as we
Walked quietly to our camp.

Lovely as the sun they welcomed,
Always greeting us with namaste,
They sometimes would ask for a pen,
Wanting an implement to
Enhance their learning.
Who would want to deprive them of this?

A Narration Of The Old City

A little train climbs the hill
At the end of my street.
In the afternoon it drowns out
The voices of the people outside
At the restaurant, between which times
They buzz at a steady pace
Interrupted frequently with
Interjections and laughs and
Exclamations, roars and proclamations.

At the other end is a café where
We eat sometimes musing at Cathedral St. Pierre,
Listening to its chimes, and the
Ringing of its bells. A little man
Climbs the myriad steps each Saturday
To play the carillon, which concert
I rather like.
Sometimes a speaker of wide repute
Will come, like the Dalai Lama
Who I heard from my room
One Sunday morning.

A New Beginning

I practiced my part in the
Ballet in the driveway behind
Your house on the terraces
Above which, twenty years later,
We celebrated your graduation
From college and engagement
At tables with wine and toasts.

If Sarah or Jack weren't there
I even asked to play with you
Hoping you might show me your
Chemistry set and your miniature safe.
Who knew you would open a bank
In Portugal and as your mother said,
"Put out a shingle as an economics
Professor at Princeton"?

The day I found out you were
Moving to our neighborhood I was
Four and was waiting for mother
To finish garden club, sitting in your
Basement with the TV on, fending off
Jack who put a banana on his head
As a wig, dancing about the room.

At The Ballet School

The music soared through the halls,
The rooms, and the offices in which
We carried on the best we could,
Wanting to fly with it, wherever,
And we did so, in the large rooms
With the mirrors and barres.

No matter the teachers rued
The sometime slowing or quickening
Rhythm of the pianists, we exuded
The breath and depth of their
Music copiously in each infinitesimal
Movement of our corps and limbs
Extending into space the science
Of our souls.

We were bold and strong, lithe and quick,
Capturing and expressing grace in
Astonishing leaps and bounds
To behold and impress the stars.

Taking Care Of Two

You were thought of as a conqueror
Of the mountains,
So I was taken by surprise
When you began to crumble,
On the descent from the last peak.

I administered your antibiotics
The whereabouts of which you described
In a barely decipherable whimpering midst wails.
When your mad rambling quieted
Despite my own inordinate
Fear of darkness,
I mustered up the courage to descend
To the stream, brave the bears,
And gather water to cook our evening meal.

Swashbuckling

From my earliest memory of
Trying not to fall back whilst
Dipping the foot wide circle
Wand into the solution and
Blowing enough air into it to make
A perfect bubble

I progressed to the forbidden
Wondrous mysterious hitherto
Undiscovered trail around the block,
On my tricycle, arriving at the halfway point
Realizing the jeopardy of my life
If I ventured one turn further,
Yet by some miraculous sense of courage
And blind passion for discovery
Pedaling forward

To marvel at the inviting swing barely
Swaying from the towering oak up the hill
On the lawn in front of the giant house
With the gardens and barns and orchards
And fields stretching out behind

Regaling in knowing the untouched mystery
Only to find enlightenment,
In a foray which posed perilous uncertainty,
And the familiar trees and yards
Near my own house.

A Bout Of Glee

One cheerful bright summer afternoon,
When we had been admonished
To our bedrooms,
We jointly decided to have
The free-for-all bash
Of emptying the chest of drawers,
Rapturously throwing all our clothes
From the second story
Onto the lawn,
Shouting to any and all passersby
To look at our marvelous feat.

Then we scrambled out the back door.

The whereabouts of my accomplice unknown,
Katie the housekeeper scooped me up
From the end of the garden walk,
Carrying me over outstretched arms
To the house, as I looked
Into her eyes, singing of cockleshells
By the seashore.

Roughhousing

We had fun bouncing your little body
On the trampoline this summer,
Yet, after remarking how wonderful
It was to bounce you so high,
Uncle Jeff bounced you all the way off.

We heard a scream from the kitchen
And then crying and then your
Rush in through the door.
You scrambled onto your mom's lap.
She held you and we saw a little blood
Only where your tooth gnashed at your lip.
You were a little shaken
But were up and running soon enough.

Preparing For Church

As I turned from you in the
Smocked navy blue velvet dress
Nana sent from Paris and toddled
Towards Dad, I felt the
Excitement of an impending outing.

He buttoned the flap just below the neck
Inching us nearer to our destination.

Raemelton Elementary School

The yellow fields stretched out
On over the plains from our windows
In the early fall and sometimes
We could smell
The fresh cut hay
Coming through.

Sometimes we watched the wind
Rippling through the tall grasses,
Some of which we would play our games on,
The others which we would only watch from afar
Wondering what it would be like
To be midst their eternity,
To the woods through the corn.

Sometimes the doors at the entrance
Were propped open,
And we heard the singing of insects.

It was a womb that held us for awhile.

Between Terms

Greenhouses steamed as
I walked among the orchids,
Spotting just the right one for my camera.
They were amongst the stables
And the garage whose chauffeur
Ran off with the proprietor's wife.

Browsing on the outskirts of
The gardens along the paths
In the woods I was aware
The country stretched out
Immensely at one time where
One meandered on a horse for a long stretch.
The cicadas chanted more intensely
In my ears as I approached
The main house,
Passing by the duck pond
Encountering peacocks and a turkey
With whom I had a stare-down
Who left wandering, jutting his head
Back and forth.

A Summer Production

In the small amphitheater
On a hill in the woods
Down from the house
I danced in a masque
In a Shakespeare play.

We sprung down the
Side stairs and unfolded
In a pleasing formation
At the back of the stage
Before the ferns in front of the
Ensuing grove of trees.

A trio of instruments accompanied us
Predominant among which sang the violin.
During this moment
With the stars overhead and the grass underfoot
We continued
With the crickets and all other nightlife
Echoing in our ears.

Prelude To A Repast

Before dinner you played
The theme song from *Felix the Cat*
At which I fulminated
In the darkness in the
Overstuffed chair by the fireplace.

You wore a shirt with little fishes
Swimming in seaweed
Tucked into black jeans.

Your face was lit up but you had no tail.

Possible Amusement

You did admit to
Knowing how to rig the tiny sailboat,
Which excited my desire
To visit and take it out
A few times.

We didn't get that far
But made for our excitement
In marrying and having
Our own families
And all the little essays
That sally forth from such.

In Off The Field

Around about the time
When the injured bat
From the silo of the farm above our houses
Lay immobile in the yard,
And we stood remarking it
In a circle at our feet,
In a prolonged inquiring daze
The neighbor boy whose yard we were in
Exclaimed "fuck" and wouldn't
Stop long enough on his bicycle
To explain it to me.

Later in mother's bathtub
I leaned over the rim asking
Her the definition and upon hearing
A very scientific yet graphic
Explanation began to sob
Which she took for laughter
Hence commencing to sob too.
Coming to realize I was not laughing
But crying because my little bubble
Was punctured, this physical act
Not being a part of my future plans
Hitherto formulated of all seven years,
Violently set ajar with this imparting,
Our miscommunication cleared,
And she imparted the notion to me
Of this act being sacred.

An Anomaly

Though Pee Wee was a champion swimmer
I didn't even make the team,
Considering all the years
My fervent pedaling on the twenty-four inch
Brought me to the swim club
Each summer.

One bathing suit was woolish
Split in two, the upper half red,
The lower blue, down which four
White stripes ran
Ending in arrow tips.

On the rare occasion it rained,
I would tentatively
Browse and poke about the den,
Sometimes with calm,
Clad only in a suit,
Anticipating and waiting
For the rain to stop
And the sun to stay out.

A Continual Spell

You were as enchanting
As the wizard of Oz
But real and more luscious
As I could make you smile,
Crawling up on your lap
To lie flat out,
Receiving the palm of your hand
Over my back.

For a moment
Eternity held us suspended in ecstasy
And nary a worry or care entered our realm,
And then my parents took me home.

In the days to come
Nana watched me haul out the toys
From the toy closet near her chair
From which I set up a tightrope
To the couch armrest and balanced
The clown on the unicycle back and forth.

In those days of my wee years
Your majesty was most encompassing
Yet provided me with a humble dignity.

The Music Pad

Among all the millions of
Sperm out there
You appeared and when
We met last summer,
A few months over one year old,
You wallowed on
The plastic electric keyboard,
Your face lit in one big spark
And your eyes rolling.

Just to hear one note after
The other in no special order
Was enough to set us all laughing
In your house by the forest.

Out Of The Cold

We visited the farm
Where Grandma grew up
Last summer and even though
There was ample land,
One could only understand
How she quit going to school
After a few years,
With no shoes on her bare feet
In winter.

The little one-room schoolhouse
Is just up and across the street
From the neatly painted house
With a picket fence in front
And a big barn further on.

In the last house I knew Grandma in
A cornered mirror with shelves
Hosted different perfume bottles
Above the big bed by the window
Which I approached sinking into the
Bed corner when no one knew my whereabouts,
Rapt in analyzing one or two carefully,
In a globe, cautious, lest it be pierced unexpectedly.

Moving Out

One afternoon, as the weather
Was turning cool,
We stopped to visit Grandma
Whom we found on a ladder,
Midst the cherry tree
Picking for a cherry pie.

Her backyard, exotic as it was,
Always induced me to
Contemplate the characters
Of her neighbors, especially
Of a boy a few years my elder.

Although time all but impregnable
At this point, Grandma pottering
In her garden was enough to set
Me a wondering about the area
Beyond her fence, and if and how
Far beyond it were wild and tame.

Homecoming

He returns at night
To wooden recorders and journals
Arranged neatly on the shelves,
The piano on the far window,
The miniature stuffed friends
In the bedroom, sometimes
Alternately waiting on his pillow.

These creatures are Badger,
With the pocket watch chain
Draped across his tummy,
Ratty, who is always a gleeful soul,
Mole, whose mirth is perpetual,
And Toady, who seems really content
To come home and rest quietly
After all from various pursuits
Ventured upon with great abandon.

It is only a short while after
When naked under the covers,
His breathing fuses with the night sounds
Of the birds, far-off cars and planes
And insects coming in through the windows.

Accent

Under the overcast winter sky
I came upon a most singular
Painting in the rounds
As a guard at the museum.

In the middle of a snow-laden field
Under a gray dreary sky
Where the dark snow met the horizon
Stood a tiny black furry skinny devil,
Upright, poising a trident, as if
Ready to strike.

Forests bordered each side
Of the field,
And it was only after closer
Inspection that one discovered
This minute surprise.

Short And Longer Sketches

Fall was in the air again
And I was naked posing
For the art students
As the sun cast large rectangles
About us.

We broke those lines,
Some working furiously,
Others at a slower pace.
As the afternoon wound down,
I anticipated walking home
Through the crisp air.

In A Prism

Not paying too much attention
To the houseware surrounding me,
I walked casually through the department
Until reaching the end of the floor
Opening out to the mall,
Whereupon I took a double glance,
Stopped, and walked into the
Wondrous globe of the New Year's eve
Table you had set with crystalware.

Crystal soup bowls set on crystal
Dinner plates and crystal stemware
Adorned each corner: a wine,
Champagne, and water glass.
Each setting had a tiny crystal clock
And decorative and functional crystal
Filled the center.
Miniature champagne glasses were
Set in various receptacles,
All of which was sprinkled with
Red, yellow, blue, and white confetti dots.

Ferry Capsule

A long pink Cadillac pulled up
In front of the children's home
By the maven of the old elite
One dark winter's Saturday morning
To take me to a ski race further north.

The charity of Frannie
Was unusual and awed me to the
Point of not being too articulate
During our prowl on
The narrow icy roads,
Even with her daughter
In the back with me.

The event of the meet was
Not exactly dashing
But in some inexplicable recess
I knew I participated in
The required roster of races,
And there was a glamorous tank
To ferry me back.

Upon The Moors

Maybe being locked up in a prison
In Annemasse across the border
From Switzerland was a result
Of my youthful over absorption
To be planted and enveloped
In some romantic European wilderness.

The fog swathed our tower
And I only had to gaze out the window
To see it slowly rising and swirling
To our floor and those above.

My space was on a mattress,
A little ways from the foot
Of the beds of my two cellmates,
Near the table and chair where
They brought me meals.

The girls seemed happy enough
Knitting and turning the TV on often.
Although happy to be leaving
After three days, I rued missing
The chance to eat the attractive
Large apple tart the whole block
Sat down to in the hall
As I strolled down the corridor
To my release.

The Peccary Of Battersea

From the bathtub I inquired
Into the adjoining room
If the steppe had been hospitable
As the host to one of your
Unpredictable nocturnal ramblings.

You seemed speechless,
Unraveled on the bed.
And not offering any reply,
I surmised the foray
Had been all absorbing,
Leaving you somewhat deflated
And in a reverie unreceptive
To investigation.

Innocent Flower Planting

Like some Herculean star
You heaved the massive spike
And pounded it into the ground
So I could plant the crocus
And tulip bulbs in the holes.

Being the only implement we found,
It conjured our hunter-gatherer instinct
And as you hurtled it over your shoulder,
Like a lissome javelin,
Throwing it through the air,
I knew the finesse of the century
Was not lost as it landed.

Tingling

As the chairlift brought me
Near the top of the hill,
I wished to penetrate
The mystery of the shadows
Of each tree trunk
In the surrounding forests.

Even more, the trees on
The backside presented
A virgin territory
Waiting to be sounded.

The night, the snow, the lights
And the moon sparkled on
As I continued up and down the hills
Sometimes gliding near the edge of a wood
Or stopping to listen and see over the land,
Wondering and sensing the singularity
Of my whereabouts, so unfettered.

Worth My While

After catching me at odd moments
And knocking at my door at all hours,
After sprawling on the bench
Between the girls' and boys' dorms
Making me hold your head in my lap
While you sobbed uncontrollably,
I accepted you into my life.

Not long after, we would climb
To the mountain pastures and
Run down ridges leaping long distances
From rock outcrops
Catching our ways with cameras,
And exhausted at day's end
Fall asleep,
Starting over in the morning
Full of wonder and glee.

You were my cozy chest to nestle in
And my arms sometimes held you
As crying, you thought I might go away.

Millennium Pixitude

You sparkled across from me
At the table where everyone's
Eyes alit upon entering,
In your long sleeve black and white
Tuxedo shirt and jacket tee shirt
Sporting a white carnation
Imprinted on the lapel.

We finished our white chocolate mousse
Wrapped in an open dark chocolate tower
With "Happy Year 2000" written in white,
Bid our friends adieu, and darted
Home in our black convertible sports car,
With the top down.

As you orchestrated the bottle rockets
In our driveway, the oversize shorts you
Put on on our return fell, and even though
You called to me to notice your white
Underwear, you would not let me photo
You as such, pulling them up before I
Could administer the camera.

We drank a little toast and before the
New Year officially rang in,
You were cocooned in the many blankets
With just your newly shorn now little head
Poking out sleeping quietly.

Arighting A Vision

After seeing the new
Waterford crystal ball drop,
You moseyed on to the
Bedroom commencing the
Wrapping of your web
Out of which shortly thereafter,
I espied your little
Head sleeping soundly.

Outing

As if discovering a further reach
Of my soul,
I ventured past the two blocks
To where the woods and fields
Stretched out awhile,
And rambled barefoot under the trees
On the paths where light
Was let in but little,
Coming out into a clearing,
Wading across the tall hay expanse
That pricked my legs,
In the afternoon of a summer
Hours from blending into evening.

The cow barn not far off,
I pried open the bull barn.
Instead of standing unafraid
Admiring the horses in their stalls,
I stood riveted in fear
At huge dangerous animals
Built to unleash their rage,
Marveling at their existence
In such close proximity
To the pillow I so peacefully
Laid my head each night,
Upon going to sleep.

Slaking Wandering

The only problem with civilization,
Is that you can't walk out
Your backdoor and keep walking,
Nevermore to meet another village.

Knowing this, where do we head
Emerging out the door
Of an afternoon,
The sun shining bright,
And the air fine,
Coursing in our blood?

It is not far to the beach
Where the ocean roars quietly
Up to our feet on the sand;
Or to the expanse of the botanical garden,
Where we might roam among the iguana
If we are brave enough
To meet the resident alligator
Lying in wait, ready to pounce;
Or even to the other shore
To walk among the deeper mangroves
And muse upon a longer, whiter water's edge.

There are areas to wander through yet,
Day after day,
Field after field,
Along ridges down into valleys,
In the lusting and fulfilling of which
My thirst is quenched
And I return through my backdoor.

What If There Had Been A Fire?

After riding the train
All day and into the night
From London I pierced the darkness
Walking up a cobble street a ways
In Glasgow, and too frightened
To proceed further, turned,
Hightailing back to the station
Whereupon a well-rounded tidy
Stationmaster unlocked the salon
Indicating a couch for me
To sleep on, which I did.

He locked the door behind him,
Opening it in the early morning.

The Letward Isle

We had discussed your wand
Last night adrift upon our bed,
It being of a black metallic tube
With a star at the end.

This came about upon my statement
That I had arranged
Your little white gloves earlier,
In the top drawer of the chest.

Whether you will be casting
Any spells in the near future
Will remain for us to discover.

Fête

In the twilight of my heyday
Before classes begin,
I saw as you passed into the room
From the bathroom
Your face blend into Badger's snout
Who sat on the windowsill
By our bed, waiting,
Ready at a moment's notice
To be called into action
To perform whatever asked.

Pushing the lawnmower,
You appeared in different
Window frames throughout the house
In no particular order
As little surprises tucked
Into the afternoon.

Two Small Brothers At Shaska Beach

Upon the sandy shores of Lake Erie
We walked, you two so little,
You still needed to be watched.
I rolled up your pants
Just before you walked into the water,
Which made you all the more in awe
Of your new surroundings,
Your eyes wide open, sensing the great space.

In the lovely loaned cottage,
We stayed for three days
And I was able to be the protector
Over all your little ramblings,
Sallying and musings.

New Ground

Passing by the stable
I stopped and entered,
Walking over the stone cobbles
In my knee-high black leather boots.

Horses on either side of the aisle
Variously eating from the mangers,
Sipping from their water buckets,
Standing with their backs turned
Or facing out,
Seemed not to mind being
In the middle of the summer day.

Having tacked up TJ
We set out eastward along the path
Behind the house that led into the wood,
Crossed back westward and traversed
The old polo field,
Crossing a few fields into the next wood.
We made a loop, coming back further
South along the vast terrain
That stretched out forever
Through the hay mounds and forests
Up above the timberline on the ridges
Down into the yonder vales
Across the brooks and roaring rivers
To a point never reached before,
A vista new to my eyes.

Penetrating

Passing by the chicken farm,
On the road between the coops
And gardener's small one-room shack
I gazed at the main red brick house,
Contentedly walking into the forest
Still on the road of smooth dirt.

Pines rose to the right,
Increasing my enchantment
As I reached the middle of the allée
And reaching the fork,
Took the western prong,
Whereupon reaching the middle,
The trees thinned
And yellow glistening hayfields emerged
On either side,
The cow pastures and farm straight ahead.
Reaching the end of this lane
I rested my head and elbows on the fence
Wondering if any bulls lurked
And after a generous moment
Made my way south again
Which led to the fields behind the house
In front of which I swayed on a
Tree swing for the better part of an hour.

Before A Great Vat

As I came out of the trees,
Tapped with sap dripping into buckets,
A large cauldron six times my height in length
And twice as high as I
Came into view in the opening of the barn doors
Bubbling over a bright fire
The length of its bottom.

So little was I compared to this great mass
That I stood still a few moments
Wondering at the bucolic glory
Of such a fantastic event.

The skies were gray
Although it was only early afternoon.
Snow lay several inches thick on the ground
And out of the mist in the clearing
The great iron bed burned on,
Hissing, crackling, and steaming,
Permeating the environs with the
Scent of maple syrup.

Exmoor

We walked out the garden gate,
Saddled up, and proceeded southwest
Upon the moors, sometimes sauntering
Sometimes galloping at full force
Until we reached the destination for lunch,
Sometimes a farmhouse,
Sometimes an inn,
Where we devoured the meal rapaciously.

Veering northward we charged
Straight on, the Bristol Channel
On the horizon, and looked into Wales.
Through the forest we pioneered,
Winding through tiny village
After tiny village, whereupon
Reaching the moors again, we spotted
Wild ponies, running from us, or with us.

After five days we came full circuit,
Arriving to a fully prepared tea.

The Texture Of Winter

Upon finishing my polo lesson at Cornell,
Preparing for the team's match,
I returned at night to my composer
Who was at his score, writing away.

On Saturdays we walked to the practice rooms,
Where he coached me dramatically
Through *Happy Birthday Cecilia*
With great verve, enthusiasm, and command.

I wore little white gloves
To a concert one night, sitting between
Him and his teacher,
Listening to the music of his colleagues.

We talked a few moments afterwards
With his teacher
And headed home,
Whereupon I resumed
My painting classes
The following Monday,
Wondering if we might ever
Go skating at the ice rink on the hill.

My Sailor Coming Home to Me

I sprinted along the sea wall
One afternoon after the hustle of classes,
Over the bridge across the Severn,
And back to the archaic cluster
Of buildings where I slept.

Amid jostling the proposition
Of waiting on the tables at Senior Dinner
And homework assignments
I migrated to the sprawling shade tree
Down from the dining hall,
Lolling with others.

It was only awhile thereafter
Whence surfaced a young man
With blond hair and twinkling blue eyes,
Profuse freckles and ruddy demeanor,
Opening his smile that beamed
On me forever afterwards.

Amid The Land

I sat on the lush grassy knoll
Up from the indoor riding arena
Looking out across the land
One late summer afternoon,
Seeing the wheat fields ripple,
The gnarly odd trees, the woods
And a few chimney tops,
Feeling the wind brush gently across my face.

The fall would be here soon enough
And there would be such things
To fill my mind as classes
And various other activities
Crowding upon each other
But I had a moment yet,
In a half carved out place,
In a land still somewhat virgin
Observing as far as my eye would allow
Where I was yet unpressed,
Regaling and supreme
In untouched glory.

Christmas In New Orleans

While it was winter break at Tulane
We went and chanted at the
Buddhist ashram,
Your mother and I,
Waiting for you to come back from school.

Many an afternoon I walked
Across the campus in riding attire
Through Audobon Park among peacocks
To the stable and a lesson.

We nestled into the living room
On Prytania, sleeping on cushions
From the furniture to the rapid
Meter of Anna's typing.

I took the trolley all the way down St. Charles
To get my inoculations for Africa spring term,
Looking towards Mardi Gras
When we could see each other again.

You told me you used to
Climb the trees in the park,
Spending hours upon hours
Playing the recorder high in their branches.

We played many games with
A miniature card deck,
In a booth in a bar
Teeming with revelers.

Our Paths Meet

You and your sisters
Climbed over the mountains from Germany
Into Austria to find your parents
Who were in Linz
Whom you had not seen for three years,
And you were put in jail for a week at the border.

I know you kept your sisters
In good spirits, which is your nature,
And your appreciation for all the
Food you had while detained was keen.

Even though you had money
It is a miracle you found your parents,
Your father preaching in the apostolic church,
And the harmless pride you share with us.

We laugh together
Seeming so morally upright,
Having both been in jail.

Your family finally
Made the crossing to America,
Whereupon, shamelessly,
You provided great support to me
From when I first entered this world
Throughout my life:
A source of great spiritual joy
Which I tap at this time.

Upon Reaching Home

I took the rickety train
At night after ballet school,
From the station downtown
Out to Shaker Square onto which
I alighted in the balmy autumn air.

Sometimes I returned from class
In the middle of the bright crisp day,
Aglow, sallying across the square
Slow and lithe
With a giant and enduring pride;
In the ableness of my body,
In being alive in those days,
And ready to make a mark
Exploring unknown places throughout the world.

Plus, I rejoiced in hoeing
A garden of talents I could
Gather from and add to in the years to come.

The Reward Of Risk

Being on the second story
Of the open air gazebo for two days,
With you in the middle of the woods
On your land is indelible in my mind.

No one knew where we were,
We had disappeared.

It was a tiny bit savage,
Seemingly problematic
Whether I would be able to return
To civilization wherein
I could participate in the hunt,
Continue ballet,
And master several languages,
Not knowing these two places
Were not mutually exclusive.

It was a leap coming out
And the time I spent with you
Although at first glance untamed,
Does have its place
And I pray, will weave itself into
The threads of the fabric of my life
Unignored and be one more seed
Among all the others
That bears fruit
From the risk taken
By the swerve from an existence
Of other people's expectations
Of a wholly different color.

Across The Hayfields

After a year on the cheerleading squad,
And a summer with few frills,
I landed in the children's home
Where I came to appreciate
Hitherto invisible frills.

Under heavy security,
On the site where
Once stood a Gothic building,
Which had little cells
Which had slots under little windows
In the doors through which food passed,
I forged many satisfying friendships,
And obtained permission for walks
With a certain small time limit
From the houseparents
And from my caseworker to
Attend a concert with friends.

Consistent in my schoolwork
The year came to an end,
And I returned home
To wait out the summer.

All types of gents came around
Calling, many of whom
Three summers earlier
Tackled me to the ground ruthlessly
After the baseball game
We played in together,
Grabbing feels of my breasts and vagina.

I must not have forgotten this,
As although I sported around
With them, some in their fancy cars,
And even became physically tender with one,
I never maintained a valued friendship.

One vying for my attention
In these goings about
Pulled a more sincere chord,
As he had not participated
In the mauling, and although
We went out to the country
And visited each other,
He was an alcoholic
Incapable of treating me decently.
Recovered, I send him a note now and then.

There was a certain comedy
In the surprise appearances
We made before each other,
Usually in my neighborhood,
And a certain gentleness,
Whose depths we plummeted
Always uncovering new layers.

At summer's end
As the hay's scent seeped
Throughout the area,
And my parents' consternation
Fraught with tears,
I was finally let loose
To go to school far away from home.

Suspended

On a round of enamel
Encased in gold
My three-year-old
Portrait was painted,
Which dangled from your wrist
At various functions and parties,
Along with those of my three brothers.

Never did I imagine
My little image
Would flash in front of strangers
Accompanying a glass to the mouth,
An hors d'oeuvre, or searching
Out the perfect crudité
To dip in an attractive sauce
On a finely laid table
Heads away from the dance floor.

I have traveled in some remote places
But none so far away
As where you took me
With this little charm.